NORTHUMBERLAND SLS	
3201833289	
Bertrams	17/08/2009
S551.5	£12.99

OUR ANGRY PLANET

Hurricanes

JEN GREEN

Adapted from an original text by Anne Rooney

FRANKLIN WATTS
LONDON • SYDNEY

First published in 2009 by Franklin Watts

Franklin Watts
338 Euston Road
London NW1 3BH

Franklin Watts Australia
Level 17/207 Kent Street, Sydney, NSW 2000

Produced by Arcturus Publishing Limited,
26/27 Bickels Yard, 151–153 Bermondsey Street, London SE1 3HA

Our Angry Planet is based on the series *Nature's Fury*, published by Franklin Watts.

Editor: Alex Woolf
Designer: Mind's Eye Design and Mike Reynolds

Picture Credits
Corbis: 4 (Mike Theiss/Jim Reed Photography), 5 (Bettmann), 6 (Reuters), 8 (NASA), 9 (Eric Nguyen/Jim Reed Photography), 13 (David Tulis), 15 (Matthew Cavanaugh/EPA), 17 (Will and Deni McIntyre), 18 (NASA/JPL-Caltech), 19 (Rick Wilking/Reuters), 20 (Richard Carson/Reuters), 23 (Reuters), 24 (John Heseltine), 25 (Rafiqur Rahman/Reuters), 27 (Jim Edds/Jim Reed Photography), 28 (David J. Phillip/Pool/Reuters).
NASA Visible Earth: 11 (Jacques Descloitres, MODIS Rapid Response Team, NASA/GSFC), 26 (Scott Dunbar, NASA JPL), 29.
Science Photo Library: 7 (NASA), 10 (NOAA), 12 (Carl Purcell), 14 (Mike Theiss/Jim Reed Photography), 16 (Jim Reed).
TopFoto: 21, 22.
Shutterstock: cover (Michelle Pacitto).

A CIP catalogue record for this book is available from the British Library.

Dewey Decimal Classification Number: 551.55'2

ISBN 978 0 7496 9049 6

Printed in China

Franklin Watts is a division of Hachette Children's Books, an Hachette UK Company
www.hachette.co.uk

Contents

What is a
Hurricane?

Hurricanes are huge spinning storms that strike in warm, **tropical** areas. They can smash buildings and hurl cars through the air. The winds in a hurricane may blow at more than 250 kilometres per hour.

▼ Sand whirls through the air as Hurricane Katrina strikes Texas in southern USA, in 2005.

Storm damage

Hurricanes begin out to sea. When they reach the coast they bring very heavy rain and thunderstorms. They can do terrible damage to seaside towns and villages. They usually die down quite quickly as they head inland.

Hurricane names

Hurricanes go by different names in different parts of the world. In the Atlantic Ocean they are called hurricanes. In parts of the Pacific they are known as **typhoons**. In India and Australia they are called **cyclones**. Tropical storms with winds of more than 118 kilometres per hour are classed as hurricanes, cyclones or typhoons.

Angry gods

In days gone by, people used to believe that hurricanes were a sign that the gods were angry. The word *hurricane* comes from Hurakán, a god of wind and storms in Central America.

▲ **In 1900 a hurricane and high seas wrecked the port of Galveston in southern USA.**

CASE STUDY

Galveston, 1900

The port of Galveston, Texas, was built on an island off southern USA. In 1900 a hurricane blew in from the ocean. A **storm surge** swept right over the island. The entire town was wrecked and over 6,000 people died. It was the worst natural disaster in US history.

Where do **Hurricanes** Strike?

Hurricanes strike in warm parts of the Atlantic, Pacific and Indian Oceans. The water temperature must be at least 26.5°C for a hurricane to form. Hurricanes do the worst damage in areas where many people live.

Storm zones

In the Atlantic Ocean most hurricanes form off the coast of West Africa. Then they drift west to hit land in Central America, the Caribbean and southern USA. In the Pacific they often strike Japan, eastern China and the Philippines. In the Indian Ocean they most often hit Indonesia, India, Sri Lanka and Thailand.

▼ **People wade through a flood in East Africa following a hurricane.**

Worst record

In the western Pacific, the Philippines and nearby islands are hit by more hurricanes than any other place on Earth. Around ten violent storms hit these islands every year.

Reaching land

After reaching land a
hurricane quickly loses power.
This is because it is no longer
heated from below by warm
ocean water. Hurricanes can
travel up to 28 kilometres
inland. But they usually die
out within 12 hours.

HURRICANES IN SPACE

Earth is not the only planet to have hurricanes. The
planet Jupiter has a huge red spot, which is actually a
massive storm. It measures 24,800 kilometres across.
Its winds spin at 400 kilometres per hour. Jupiter is
made entirely of gas, so the storm will never move over
land and die down.

▲ Jupiter's red spot is a
giant storm. It has been
raging for at least 300
years.

How do **Hurricanes** Begin?

Hurricanes begin out at sea where winds blow together from opposite directions. Warm air starts to spiral upwards. The storm grows stronger as it is fed by heat and moisture from the sea.

▼ **This picture was taken by a satellite. It shows a tropical storm forming in the Caribbean.**

Power from the sea

Hurricanes begin as thunderstorms over warm oceans. The storm contains swirling clouds and bands of rain. Winds blow at up to 62 kilometres per hour. Warm, moist air rises from the sea surface. The air cools as it rises and its moisture **condenses** – turns to tiny water drops. These gather to form clouds.

Circling winds

Heat is released as moisture condenses. This makes the winds spiral upwards ever faster. In turn, this sucks more air and moisture from the surface of the sea.

Above the storm, winds carry the warm air away. This draws up more air from below. The winds spin faster and faster. Finally they reach hurricane force – over 118 kilometres per hour.

◄ A tornado destroys a house in southern USA in 2004. This was a record year for tornadoes.

 TORNADOES

Tornadoes are small, violent **whirlwinds**. They sometimes form near hurricanes, but usually they form on land. The whirling funnel of air reaches down from a thundercloud. Tornadoes can travel at 55 kilometres per hour. Winds can be even stronger than in a hurricane, spinning at 250 kilometres per hour.

Inside a **Hurricane**

All hurricanes have the same structure. Storm clouds, wind and rain spin around a calm area in the centre, called the **eye**.

Parts of a hurricane

The clouds are thickest near the centre of the storm, just around the eye. This region is called the **eyewall**. It also contains the fastest winds.

Hurricanes are huge. They can tower 18 kilometres high. A large hurricane can measure 480 kilometres across. The very biggest measure 1,300 kilometres wide.

▼ The eyewall of Hurricane Katrina, seen from inside the hurricane.

Air pressure

Air pressure is the weight of air pressing down on Earth. The pressure is not the same everywhere. Where warm air rises, it creates an area of low pressure. Winds spiralling around the eye of a hurricane make these centres of very low pressure.

Measuring hurricanes

The scale used to measure hurricanes is based on wind speed.

CATEGORY	WIND SPEEDS	DAMAGE
1	119–153 km/h	Slight damage to buildings; flooding on coasts
2	154–177 km/h	Damage to roofs, doors and windows; some trees uprooted
3	178–209 km/h	Small buildings suffer damage; large trees blown down; floods inland and on coasts
4	210–249 km/h	Small buildings lose roofs; sandy beaches swept away; floods inland and on coasts
5	Over 249 km/h	All buildings lose their roofs; some buildings destroyed; floods damage coastal buildings

▼ **Hurricane Isabel whirls across the Caribbean in 2003.**

HURRICANE WINDS

Hurricanes contain winds whirling at 160 to 250 kilometres per hour. In 2005 Hurricane Wilma gusted at 281 kilometres per hour – the most powerful Atlantic storm ever known. The worst Pacific **typhoons** contain winds of up to 320 kilometres per hour. The winds circle anticlockwise in oceans north of the equator. They circle clockwise south of the equator.

Hurricane Season

Hurricanes only form in warm, sticky weather. In the Atlantic they strike any time from early June to the end of November. This period is known as the hurricane season.

Tracking storms

Weather experts track winds and storms in an effort to spot when a hurricane is brewing. However, these storms are unpredictable. It is often difficult for scientists to tell exactly how powerful they will be when they hit the coast.

▼ **Rough seas batter Jamaica as Hurricane Gilbert hits land in 1988.**

Hurricane warning

If weather experts feel a storm could be dangerous, they tell the governments of the countries lying in its path. Governments must decide whether to tell people to take shelter where they live, or move to a safer place.

Leave or stay?

People may be ordered to leave, or **evacuate**, their homes. Long traffic jams can result if everyone tries to leave at the same time. Some storms turn out to be less powerful than experts predicted. When this happens, people may take less notice of future warnings.

HURRICANE NAMES

Hurricanes are given human names. In the Atlantic, a set of names is provided for each year – see page 30. The first hurricane of the year is given a name starting with A. The next has a name that starts with B, and so on through the alphabet. If all the names are used, the letters of the Greek alphabet are used instead.

▲ Traffic builds up as people flee from Hurricane Floyd, which hit southern USA in 1999.

Wild Winds
and **Water**

Hurricanes can wreck ships at sea. They can also threaten aircraft. But they do the most damage when they hit land. Heavy rain and high tides often cause flooding when the storm strikes the coast.

▼ People struggle against strong winds in south-east USA as Hurricane Katrina hits further along the coast.

Danger at sea

All hurricanes form out at sea. Some travel thousands of kilometres before reaching land. All ships in the area are in danger. High winds and rough seas make it very difficult for lifeboats or helicopters to rescue sailors shipwrecked by the storm.

Storm surge

The **eye** in the centre of the storm sucks up water. This creates a mound of water below the hurricane, called the **storm surge**. This acts like a very high tide as the hurricane hits land. Storm surges often wreck buildings on the coast.

Super typhoons

The most powerful Pacific hurricanes are called super typhoons. The largest ever recorded formed in 1979. Named Super Typhoon Tip, it measured 2,174 kilometres across. It contained winds of 306 kilometres per hour. Luckily, Tip never struck land.

▲ These fishing boats were washed ashore when Hurricane Katrina struck in 2005.

CASE STUDY

Hakata Bay, 1281

In 1281 Mongol leader Kublai Khan sent a fleet of ships to attack Japan. But the fleet was destroyed by a **typhoon**. In 1274 an earlier invasion had met the same fate. The Japanese believed that the gods had sent the typhoon to save them. They called it Kamikaze, meaning 'divine wind'.

The **Storm Approaches**

An approaching hurricane is scary for everyone in its path. People brace themselves for the worst storm they have ever known.

Rough seas

The **storm surge** is the first sign that the hurricane has arrived. Waves up to 13 metres high lash sea walls and spill over into harbours. Rough seas smash boats against the quay or lift them up and drop them far inland.

▶ In 1996 Hurricane Fran lashed southern USA. Shop workers prepared by boarding up shops.

The storm hits

The wind gets stronger and stronger. Rain pelts down. Howling winds uproot trees and tear roofs off houses. Cars are tossed around like toys. People, too, can be swept off their feet and hurled through the air.

Eye of the storm

After a while, the wind drops. People think the storm has passed, but in fact they are in the **eye** of the hurricane. Soon the roaring winds pick up again. The storm restarts, as terrifying as ever. People who emerge from shelter can get caught out by the second wind.

▲ Hurricane Hugo wrecked this house in south-eastern USA in 1989.

CASE STUDY

Hurricane Mitch, 1998

Hurricane Mitch struck Nicaragua, Central America, in 1998. The hurricane moved slowly, giving the region a thorough drenching. The downpour triggered floods. In hilly areas the wet ground slipped away in **landslides** and **mudflows**. Mitch killed 11,000 people. It was the deadliest Atlantic storm since the Great Hurricane of 1780.

Death and Destruction

▼ New Orleans in southern USA before Hurricane Katrina struck in 2005 (top), and after the hurricane flooded much of the city.

People fear the strong winds of a hurricane. In fact, people who die in hurricanes are most often killed by flooding or the after-effects of the storm.

High winds

When a hurricane strikes, howling winds can smash people against trees or buildings. People can also be killed by flying **debris**. Others die or are injured when buildings collapse.

Floods and landslides

Storm surges often cause flooding on coasts. Further inland, very heavy rain can make rivers burst their banks. **Landslides** and **mudflows** can sweep down from high ground to bury people alive.

After the storm

The danger is far from over even when the storm passes. People may have nowhere to shelter as the bad weather continues. Often there is not enough food or clean water. Rescue services may be unable to reach the region, so sick and injured people may not get help for days.

In camps and emergency shelters, survivors are often crowded together with little clean water. Disease can spread quickly in such conditions.

▲ This couple and their baby were stranded by floods after Hurricane Katrina hit New Orleans in 2005.

CASE STUDY

The Great Hurricane, 1780

The deadliest Atlantic storm ever was made up of three hurricanes, which hit the Caribbean in 1780. The hurricanes killed 22,000 people in eight days. They caused flooding and flattened towns on many islands. They also sank British and Dutch ships in the Caribbean.

Helping Out

When a hurricane strikes a region, rescue teams swing into action. Often, local emergency services cannot cope with the demand. National and sometimes international teams are called in to help.

Cut off

Rescue workers can find it hard to reach the stricken region. **Landslides** and **debris** may block roads. Floods can sweep away roads and bridges. If strong winds continue, planes and helicopters may not be safe to use.

▼ **Survivors of Hurricane Katrina pack a sports stadium in a nearby city.**

First tasks

The first job for rescue workers is often to free people trapped in damaged buildings. People may be cut off by floods. Medical staff move injured people to safety. Dead bodies must be removed as quickly as possible. Unburied bodies can spread disease and are very upsetting to survivors.

Leaving the area

The government may decide that everyone should leave the area. People may be safer elsewhere if floods or more bad weather threaten the region. However, with roads, bridges and railways down, it may not be possible for people to leave.

▲ Rescue workers pluck a baby from a raging river after Hurricane Hortense strikes the Caribbean in 1996.

CASE STUDY

Hurricane Katrina, 2005

Hurricane Katrina struck New Orleans in southern USA in August 2005. Water spilled over high walls built to protect the city from flooding. Thousands of people took shelter in sports stadiums. But these often lacked electricity, **sanitation** and enough food and water. Many people felt that the US government did not handle the crisis well.

After the **Hurricane**

People start to rebuild their lives in the weeks following a hurricane. However, towns and villages have been wrecked. People have lost friends and family. Life has changed for ever.

Cleaning up

Rescue teams start to clear the **debris** from shattered buildings. Flood waters are drained or pumped away. Flood barriers are rebuilt. Buildings that are unsafe are pulled down.

▼ **This village in Bangladesh was wrecked by a cyclone in 1991.**

Roads, railways and bridges are repaired so it is easier to reach the region. Vital services such as water and electricity are restored. Local schools, hospitals and shops reopen.

Shattered lives

Many people have lost loved ones. Even more have lost their homes. For all these people, life will never be the same.

Rebuilding

Most people want to stay in the area they call home. But rebuilding homes so they will be storm-proof is expensive. In poor countries, homes are just patched up. These homes will be at risk if a hurricane strikes again one day.

▲ Fire burned down this man's beach house after Hurricane Claudette struck southern USA in 2003.

CASE STUDY

Bangladesh, 1970

In 1970 the deadliest **cyclone** of the 20th century struck East Pakistan, near India. This region is now called Bangladesh. Between 300,000 and 500,000 people died. Very powerful winds wrecked coastal towns. The River Ganges flooded a huge area. Most people in Bangladesh are poor and live in areas at risk of flood.

Effects on Nature

Hurricanes kill and injure people and wreck homes. They also damage the natural world in ways that affect people in the months and years ahead.

Farms and forests

Hurricanes can destroy fields and orchards that provide food. They can wreck forests that provide timber. Farms and forests can also be damaged by floods, especially if the water is salty. If the whole harvest is lost, people can starve. Farm animals are also killed by winds or floods.

▼ **These trees were uprooted by a severe storm that hit southern Britain in 1987.**

Fishing and tourism

In rivers and coastal seas, fish and shellfish can be killed by hurricanes. Local fishermen may be unable to catch food. Seaside towns that rely on tourism can be very badly affected. The area has to be cleared up quickly or tourists will desert the region. That will put people out of work.

Pollution

Hurricanes can damage factories and oil refineries. Out at sea, oil tankers may be thrown onto rocks or sandbanks. Oil or chemicals may start to leak onto the land or into the water. Wildlife can be harmed by this **pollution**.

◄ A boy helps his goat to safety during a flood in Bangladesh in 2004.

CORAL REEFS AT RISK

Coral reefs that grow in **tropical** seas can be badly damaged by hurricanes. Pounding waves break off bits of coral. The pieces may be hurled against other reefs to damage them too. Soil washed into the sea by floods can smother coral. Pollution can upset the delicate balance of the reef.

Watching for Hurricanes

▼ **This image was made using radar equipment. It shows the speed and direction of winds inside a hurricane.**

Weather experts keep a close eye on sea and wind conditions in an effort to predict hurricanes. But even using modern technology, it is difficult to predict the exact size and strength of storms.

Danger signs

Instruments called tide **gauges** check for rising sea levels that suggest a storm is brewing. Wind gauges measure wind speeds. Satellites track storm clouds as they drift across oceans. Information from all these sources is fed into powerful computers. These help scientists to predict the size of storms and where they will hit land.

Getting ready

When a storm is due, people prepare for the worst. On coasts in Australia and southern USA, many homes have storm shutters fitted to windows. Some people have built-in shelters, which provide safety in bad storms.

In some areas hurricane drills are held in schools, homes and work places. People practise what to do in a hurricane so they will be ready if a real storm strikes.

▲ A hurricane hunter flies into Hurricane Ophelia in 2005.

HURRICANE HUNTERS

Hurricane hunters get a thrill from seeing storms at close quarters. These pilots fly their planes close to storms and even enter the **eye** and fly along inside it. Research planes fly above storms and drop instruments attached to parachutes. The instruments measure wind speeds and other conditions as they drop through the clouds.

Trouble Ahead

▲ **Much of New Orleans had to be rebuilt following Hurricane Katrina.**

Since the 1990s there have been many powerful hurricanes. These **tropical** storms seem to be striking more often. Some experts believe they will become even more common in future.

Warming seas

Hurricanes only form over warm seas. Scientists have discovered that the oceans are getting warmer because temperatures are rising worldwide. This problem is called **global warming**.

What causes global warming?

Scientists believe that global warming is being caused by air **pollution**. As we burn oil, coal and gas for energy, we release carbon dioxide and other waste gases. These gases build up in the **atmosphere**. They are trapping the Sun's heat near the Earth. This is probably causing the warming.

Risk of floods

As the world warms, ice in the polar regions has started to melt. This is swelling the water in the oceans and making sea levels rise. In future, flooding may become more likely on coasts – particularly when a hurricane strikes. Some areas seem to be getting more rain, which adds to the risk of floods.

NEW HURRICANE ZONE?

In 2004 the first hurricane ever recorded in the South Atlantic struck the coast of Brazil. Scientists were alarmed by this event. Many put the blame on global warming. No one knows whether hurricanes will now become more common in the South Atlantic. Perhaps this was a one-off disaster.

▲ This map shows sea temperatures around the globe. Hurricanes form over warm seas, shown in red and yellow.

TEN OF THE DEADLIEST HURRICANES, CYCLONES AND TYPHOONS

When	Where	Casualties
1970	Bangladesh	300,000–500,000
1881	Haiphong, Vietnam	300,000
1737	Calcutta, India	Up to 300,000
1876	Bay of Bengal	200,000
1991	Bangladesh	138,000
1882	Mumbai, India	100,000
1864	Calcutta, India	70,000
1281	Hakata Bay, Japan	45,000–65,000
1780	Martinique, St Eustatius and Barbados (Great Hurricane)	22,000
1998	Nicaragua and Honduras (Hurricane Mitch)	11,000

HURRICANE NAMES

The following names have been allocated to hurricanes in the North Atlantic for the years 2009–2013.

2009	2010	2011	2012	2013
Ana	Alex	Arlene	Alberto	Andrea
Bill	Bonnie	Bret	Beryl	Barry
Claudette	Colin	Cindy	Chris	Chantal
Danny	Danielle	Don	Debby	Dorian
Erika	Earl	Emily	Ernesto	Erin
Fred	Fiona	Franklin	Florence	Fernand
Grace	Gaston	Gert	Gordon	Gabrielle
Henri	Hermine	Harvey	Helene	Humberto
Ida	Igor	Irene	Isaac	Ingrid
Joaquin	Julia	Jose	Joyce	Jerry
Kate	Karl	Katia	Kirk	Karen
Larry	Lisa	Lee	Leslie	Lorenzo
Mindy	Matthew	Maria	Michael	Melissa
Nicholas	Nicole	Nate	Nadine	Nestor
Odette	Otto	Ophelia	Oscar	Olga
Peter	Paula	Philippe	Patty	Pablo
Rose	Richard	Rina	Rafael	Rebekah
Sam	Shary	Sean	Sandy	Sebastien
Teresa	Tomas	Tammy	Tony	Tanya
Victor	Virginie	Vince	Valerie	Van
Wanda	Walter	Whitney	William	Wendy

GLOSSARY

air pressure The pressing down of all the air in the atmosphere.

atmosphere The layer of air around the Earth.

condense When moisture in the air turns to tiny water drops.

cyclone Another word for a hurricane.

debris Rubbish and broken pieces.

evacuate Leave an area because of danger.

eye The calm area in the centre of a hurricane.

eyewall The band of thick cloud around the eye of a hurricane.

gauge A measuring instrument.

global warming Warming conditions worldwide.

landslide When soil and rock slips downhill.

mudflow When liquid mud spills downhill.

pollution Any substance that harms the natural world.

sanitation A sewage system; also public health generally.

storm surge A mound of water that forms below a hurricane.

tornado A small but powerful storm with spinning winds.

tropical Relating to the hot regions around the equator.

typhoon Another word for a hurricane.

whirlwind A spinning column of air.

FURTHER INFORMATION

Books

Extreme Weather: A Guide and Record Book by Christopher Burt (Norton, 2004)

Eyewitness Guide: Hurricane and Tornado by Jack Challoner (Dorling Kindersley, 2004)

Horrible Geography: Stormy Weather by Anita Ganeri (Scholastic, 1999)

Magic Treehouse Research Guides: Twisters and Other Terrible Storms by Will Osborne (Random House, 2003)

Websites

www.bbc.co.uk/weather/features/understanding/hurricane_cycle.shtml

www.hurricaneville.com/historic.html

kids.earth.nasa.gov/archive/hurricane/index.html

Videos/DVDs

The Day After Tomorrow directed by Roland Emmerich (20th Century Fox, 2004)

The Hurricane directed by John Ford (HBO Home Video, 1937)

Key Largo directed by John Huston (Warner Brothers, 1948)

Twister directed by Jan de Bont (Warner Home Video, 1996)

INDEX

Page numbers in **bold** refer to illustrations.